The Ohio State University Press/*The Journal* Award in Poetry

Blood Prism

Edward Haworth Hoeppner

THE OHIO STATE UNIVERSITY PRESS / COLUMBUS

Library of Congress Cataloging-in-Publication Data
Hoeppner, Edward Haworth.
 Blood prism / Edward Haworth Hoeppner.
    p. cm. — (Ohio State University Press/The journal award in poetry)
 ISBN-13: 978-0-8142-5181-2 (pbk. : alk. paper)
 ISBN-10: 0-8142-5181-1 (pbk. : alk. paper)
 ISBN-13: 978-0-8142-9273-0 (cd-rom)
 1. American poetry—21st century. I. Title. II. Series: Ohio State University Press/The
journal award in poetry.
 PS3558.O3437B56 2011
 811'.54—dc22
                              2011021051

This book is available in the following editions:
Paper (ISBN 978-0-8142-5181-2)
CD-ROM (ISBN 978-0-8142-9273-0)

Cover design by Mia Risberg
Type set in Adobe Granjon
Printed by The HF Group

9 8 7 6 5 4 3 2 1

for Louie Skipper, thirty-five years
and for Susan, as ever

Contents

Acknowledgments   ix

I. *Memory*

Trees We Thought Were Walking   3
Amish Roadway   5
Behind Clouds   6
Painting of Dunes, Left to Right   7
Loss   8
Walking at Night   9
Weathered Crèche   11
Imprint   12
On the Demise of the Poetic Apostrophe   14
On Top of Central High School in the Middle of the Night   15
No Elegy   16
Landscape with a Lake and Small Island   17
At Lourdes   18
Swimming after Nightfall   19
Something of My Mother's   20
Manchild   21
The Last Time I Saw Him I Didn't   22
Lamp and Wick   24
The Night You Thought to Stop   25
Shadow   27
The Other Biography   28
Sunburst, Rush Hour   29

II. *Politics*

Shapes as Prologue in the Tower of London   33
Hatred: On Returning to a Poem with Language Backwards   34
The Trickle of Blood   36
Teens   37
"Long War" Drone: On a Term Proposed and Abandoned by the Pentagon   38
The First of the Month   40

Drought in August   41

Smoke Love   42

Paradise   44

Cooling Tower, Smokestack   45

Wartime Portrait, Dried Sunflowers   46

High Waves   47

Blood Gutter   48

Referred Pain   49

On Sound: As Sirens in *The Diary of Anne Frank*   51

Some of Us   53

Reading Tracks in Snow   54

Wrought Iron Grapes and Leaves   55

On Reading *War and Peace*   56

Lake Fogged In   58

Abundance   59

Saint Ophelia   60

III. *Age*

Dispatch   63

Cloak   64

Ghost Pain   65

After AA, the Somnambulist Dream Again   66

Recovery   67

Mist   68

Path in Sand, with Hawthorn   69

Walking on Water   70

Torch   71

On Translucence   72

An Ordinary Day not Red   73

Terrestrial   74

Not the Quick   75

Ash   76

Lullaby   77

Shore As Body   78

Ink Drawing   79

All Souls' Morning   80

On Plato in December after Dark   81

Stippling, Winter: Letter to a Tropical Mind   82

No Postcard from a Snowfield   84

After White-Out   86

Acknowledgments

My thanks to the editors of the following publications, in which these poems first appeared:

Artisan: "Some of Us"
Crazyhorse: "Saint Ophelia" and "Trees We Thought Were Walking"
Denver Quarterly: "Ghost Pain"
Iconoclast: "Reading Tracks in Snow"
Indiana Review: "Stippling, Winter: Letter to a Tropical Mind"
The Journal: "Hatred: On Returning to a Poem with Language Backwards,"
     "Imprint," "On Top of Central High School in the Middle of the Night,"
     "The Night You Thought to Stop" and "The Other Biography"
Loonfeather: "Manchild"
Louisiana Literature: "Cloak"
New Orleans Review: "Ink Drawing"
Pegasus: "Swimming After Nightfall"
Poem: "Wrought Iron Grapes and Leaves"
The South Carolina Review: "Painting of Dunes, Left to Right"
The South Dakota Review: "Abundance"

Thanks to departmental colleagues and students of literature and writing at Oakland University (especially friends of the "poetry thief"). Thanks to Steve Fazzalare, for his poems and commentary; to Mary Reusch, for painting landscapes that poems in this book admire (such as "Painting of Dunes, Left to Right," "Landscape with a Lake and Small Island," Sunburst, Rush Hour" and "Lake Fogged In"). Great thanks to Kathy Fagan, for a gracious reading and response. For my life as a father, endless gratitude to Matthew, Elizabeth, and Luke Haworth-Hoeppner—wonders all.

I. *Memory*

Trees We Thought Were Walking

We pried the foot of this one up and
it would creak when the pup was
buried in its blue shoe box then.
Little criers, that was us. And
this one, needled,
worked as blinds for the bedroom, so
that you were always under water and
the light came down through water. There
were rooms we couldn't enter in
the house. There were houses we couldn't enter on
the street and
streets we couldn't cross,
neighborhoods of mumbling dead. Louder
voices than the ones we heard.
There was the river, there were
Bluffs and trees—elm and maple, birch and
sycamore, oak and spruce and
pine, basswood, walnut, hickory—to
the edge of both. The water walked though we would not
know much of that. But trees: *The
One to Burst in Flames,* the *Tree of
Snakes, Trees that Touched Only in
the Wind.* There was the *Tree with
Doll Faces, Three Trees Built
to Hiding* and the *Five Great Ladder Trees.* With leaves in
our faces—*dust to dust*—we said
what we had seen. There
was the *Tree That Was the
Oldest Thing,* and *Tree to Hold the Hanging Corpse.* I
thought that they could move, said things.
I was wrong. I thought they understood somehow,
somehow suffered with us. But in
patience. I was wrong. I thought they walked
among us, until the blank daylight I
was made to see. I

thought that they were trees, drew
some strength from out the earth where they were
placed, thought
their voices branched out from
their foreheads, they were not human.

Amish Roadway

A fat rain blunted

cobblestones, drops bursting into little crowns.
It was *the rain of end,* was *no princess*

rain, was *princes disappearing*
in a great deluge. There is no poverty like the smell of bread.

It was heavy, heavy rain, *trench* rain, the earth mined
as if it were wet pelvis drilled: marrow,

tiny prisons torn, *cellular rain.* Clouds went past
like shadows of the trees we drove through, strobe-light, fusing

on and off, each inflated as the rooms of childhood: the car's
back seat, *the hallway cloud, the cube of sleep*

or—as tall ships carried cannon—underneath the eaves
of every wooden barn we passed, ladders

hung and yawned.

Behind Clouds

The grownups would take the candy dish
across the carpet, into the sulky woods,

where they talked about talking.
I would sit at the edge of the sun as if.

It was no lake I could drop my feet into.
No Susquehanna rolling. But close,

close as my brother's eye when he slept
on his side in the other bed, the eye

I saw moving as a horse shivers,
but he was fast asleep and innocent.

This land is a thing I wanted, as evening
on the heels of backlit clouds, not memory:

trees that moved so far through light to here,
feeding, light and light and all day through

their leaves, calm down. Then night to ride,
a thinning. Someone else to drive.

There's the harp and there's the history of harp
making, strings flared out along the wood

curved. This and music that is possible,
made from some great pressure holding back.

Painting Dunes, Left to Right

As if the earth ran like water and it does,
sand has lapped an eon against these trees,

against the stone that rises up more slowly
from the water. That has risen.

And what would this green be, if we had no need to build our homes on it?

She toes the edge of the slope, her canvas
tipped slightly, as the chairs of old ones

at the picnic tilted, slightly, one set of legs
stuck further in the earth. They slump

a bit, like these dunes, shoulders. But sand will also climb,

it piles and builds and blows and settles
and something roots. A patch of sawgrass,

its bright blades, like emery but green,
springing off the wind, slowing it, dragging it down

like the child I was, caught up as I took the laughing stairs.

As those old ones caught her up,
once, as the caught wind pools

into shade and something—*that is
going to be a tree?*—will settle there

and push, crookedly, up and out, and always, brush-like, bent inland.

Loss

As a fine purple dust across the sand, a woman
with her arms raised, levitating
a young man, splayed like waves of heat that rise
from rock, silence takes the street
once the school bus disappears. The cabinets are open
just a crack, some trudge back to sleep,
some are shaving while a crow tacks one black glove
into the grass. I remember thinking,
when my father left for work, of danger in his absence.
But he came back, salesman
Ulysses, every evening, although I thought he might've died.
So each day the rain makes sentences
against the earth: *this and this and period; this and this and stop.*
The only money I've had to invest,
I plunked down on Western Union thirty years ago,
at the dawn of what you'd call
The Internet Age. That's me, riding my quick pony
with a missive into nowhere.
He gallops like my father's laughter, long and yellow teeth,
and I find myself this normal
morning in the drylands, clear-eyed at the message
that now he's gone he's here.

Walking at Night

A dog came into one thin cone
of streetlight. Trotted out,

erased. I could hear it for awhile and then not,
as we became the caves we were,

the cave that we were moving through,
when strings of light were snapped

so quickly out in Harmony
Cavern. And then?

Our invisible hands, a sneeze
held back, an unseen fluttering

inches from our eyes. Nothing
glowed out from dark stone.

And to see nothing move? To scan
an empty world, lifeless

as the surface of an asteroid
in movies from a NASA fly-by,

image after image, the moons of Jupiter,
each one terrible, without

the smallest alteration
or shifting, the spacecraft

sailing, a molecule across
the eye of a dead horse?

There was nothing in the darkness.
And out in that nothing, a dog

*

somewhere, the coil and rasp
of a shovel scratching gravel.

Weathered Crèche

The year-end cold wasn't deep so much as blue,
as electricity is blue, the snow-draped statues,
        as fingernails glow.
                * * *
Sonogram, they used
        noise to see if I was yet.
                * * *
In twelve years I was twelve.
        One and two.
I saw my face inside
a jar that held a fetal lamb.

You would say *it was*   *on the outside,*
        but when I put my thumb there
nothing rubbed off
        onto my thumb.
                * * *
That year a blue cop
        inked that same thumb
in case I was to be
        kidnapped.

So much for childhood . . .
                * * *
. . . I didn't see right through
        into *The Rescue.*

        I heard sirens.
I didn't see a moving star.

Imprint

What's gone is less than what's not missing yet,
the boy I was rusting in the snow,
a sharp and empty field and he is spinning fast.

What is it he was thinking?
Why's he always been alone when I bring him
back, and seems from here quite happy,

small against the white hillside? There's a sled
he's dragged, half-way
up, two pines like deep green coral,

and the sky is thick. I am
never certain why he's stopped, walked off
from the rest of memory

out onto this page, his face wrapped loosely
in a scarf that looks blue
plaid, mostly. This is how he lies, straight up,

though I can't think of this
as lying. What I can't recall is how I get him home,
curled up against the register,

cup of cocoa in his hands. Was he lost,
found crying on the slopes?
Did Kathy and her father come on time,

pick him up? I can't connect
these images and always leave him spinning there, mittens
hanging at his sleeves.

There aren't even tracks. His boots, which I see
clearly, haven't marked the field
and, even as he turns and walks, the snow is staying

empty. Say I get a bird
to cross the sky, the silhouette of my hands now.
That won't get him back.

What's left is what is always left, and why I know
this isn't simple fiction:
I cannot move him from the scene by any slick device,

the sled he's got, the rope
inside his hand. So he breaks up again, vanishes
into the cold and wind.

All I do is watch him fade, see the hillside drained of him,
before it also disappears.
How he's gone is nothing but the next thing that I'll do.

Another pot of coffee,
maybe not. And standing, undecided yet, this wooden chair.
This white rug around my feet.

On the Demise of Poetic Apostrophe

I was the sound, sleeping,
of my mother vacuuming the stairs,
the sound of her needle
stitching: *something here, something gone.*

Then, lush eyes and greener voice,
a salesman erects himself in our doorframe.
"Thing ya' gotta' have," he said.
Where you think he studied this production, "voice?"

I turned from his belt buckle, someone gone:
he'd've, we'd've, should've, didn't.

It was clear, by 1919,
one mustn't speak directly
to tree or beast or star, in poetry.

Still, my mother chatted up
her houseplants and they thrived.
Talked optimistically. My uncle fondly knocked
his stiff Ford. "You piece of junk," for instance,
a mouth stuffed with smiling wires.

It might have been the Great War.
It might have been that nothing offered talking back.

But only yesterday this Lucy, oh,
this African Gray Parrot died,
who proved her brain knew abstract thought,
tapped *I love you* and *will you
come back in the morning.* Her last words,

written down. So it's possible a hand can read
The Book of Missing Letters, even in pure darkness.

As, centuries ago, her name did mean *light.*

On Top of Central High School
in the Middle of the Night

There was a system: this red body   was scooped out.
      A woman's hands opened
      as that strange tatter of light
dropped like a feather.   There was the sewing shut.

Multiply the solo   by a thousand lockers:
      maybe anger still   whorls in the depths of halls,
and shame,   but there was so much   glow and chatter,
laughter,   plankton.   Years flutter past.

I understand there are, in some restaurants,
      chefs who will prepare a dish—sushi,
bright soufflés—just the way you ask.
      I've not met one.

But mark how all the particles keep
      moving in their unseen corridors,

mark a journey built from spines,   not this map,
      with people   always leaving, coming home.
Any glass may hold the sea.   The sun
      seems to rise, solidify a bit,   and off the flat rooftop,
stars that I could barely see   vanish and will not.

No Elegy

In a rush of April heat, memory abandons me.   There are stones
          at the river's edge, and   each is.   I can walk on them
like death across a cartoon   battlefield.

But you didn't shrink to some bad   Nike when you left,   no such *oompah!*
          You died like toothpaste,   too quickly,
like *the grandmother-who's-back-in-Ireland-and-I–never-saw.*   Now
I have to figure in my head   the years it's been.   Nothing's automatic,
          like a spruce tree grown   into the very shape its cone predicted,
grown, as crystals   do, into themselves.

There's a bird of some sort   over there and it is free.   It's a free bird.
          I take this to mean   it has its predators.
Or I can walk across these stones without   numbering: a *week*
          and *month* or *year* from *hour . . . hour . . . hour . . .* Without
" *. . . not a day goes by   without . . .* "   And so forth.

I can't remember what it was, kissing you in high school.
I know the earth was not   round it was a wave,   a warming smudge.
My shoulder was a pear and your   teeth behind.   A hurry and a muss.

But you have reigned—a fact like Pluto   (planet,
          not the dog,   underworld kingpin)—   over more than half my life:
The First Girl That I Touched.   Past   tense.   Nonetheless.
Here's a shoreline popped along with little stones I feel on the bottoms
          of my feet. Why   should they remind me now of you?

And there's a string of ants in their   manic, flat routine,   eating
          something, part divine.   That's probably not right:
          that would make them   gods themselves.

Landscape with a Lake and Small Island

Before *this,* we had the word for *you*
surrounded by still water. It stood for a while
        in dense green at the island's edge
and stared back where it came from with one hand raised.

Emigrate, we called to it, *look ahead,*
but these sounds turned aside
        from that hand and tracked into the island's heart. Water
lilies grew up in the space between us, slow

current. We thought, at first, *isolate,* but that was wrong.
There were trees across the lake, we could see,
        and one might make a living.
We thought *island* come to mean *protected, insular,*

secured. This was our mistake. The water moved
downhill as it will, from left to right
        more often than is otherwise. It carried red
into those lilies. We figured then

this could be a measure counting time. Another error.
As for the island, now? There is no news.
The water at our feet is thick and blue
as blood returning. Still, far off, over there,

        it flattens into *silver like a mirror.*

At Lourdes

Something's said to rise out through their flashing
School, turn water into air. Pilgrims, where is *out*

And what is *it?* Delusion? Disbelief?
First there were the closets, then this forest,

Of crutches, canes. I put my hand where others have:
On one bronze foot, worn down to a feather.

Swimming after Nightfall

and rain: *inside* water:
and, from below, on the surface: dark
bridge, fingertips,

the cool, broken *dot-to-dot*
of my mother's voice: " . . .
you are beautiful," she said and died.

This *around, around*
and *all.* This black *within.* Her praise.
My feet hanging here like noon.

Something of My Mother's

I've never worn a dress
        to the best of my knowledge, cloth with a bouquet.
I don't know what it's like wearing something so *infused*.

Half a conversation,
        maybe this one, in which I try again to have an *I,*
imagine someone there where you must be, reading over

your shoulder as well.
        But I've spent a lot of time with flowers,
noted little pinks that fade to lavender. I've tracked

leafshape back into its name
        and quiver: the family of asters, little stars with dust
so golden I have eaten it. Nonetheless,

how I got this print of hers
        I can't recall, sorted from the things that blurred
inside the smoke of grief and hurry: this pattern,

floral, convoluted, brash.
        Count the seconds: every twenty-six, a wave in any ocean
sips or overwhelms the shore. Wet clockwork.

That pulse, white-capped,
        her letters and her sifted jewelry—all things going up,
dissolved like air. This clothing. This one dress

in my closet, hanging,
        as it hung in hers, fading and delinquent, even many years
beyond the day when it last fit her well.

Manchild

My father at eighty asked me to stand so he could walk down to the lake. He turned me around when I faced him and put his hands on my shoulders lightly. We hadn't done this before.

* * * * *

I could say *like birds,* remembering exactly when his strength left him: we were hauling out the air conditioner, up the basement stairs. A light bulb swung overhead. I don't remember who brushed it. Then I felt the weight shift into me and had to quickly stop. I glanced at him. He'd nearly lost his grip. He turned his head away as if ashamed. It seemed the first time I'd looked him in the eye, though I know this isn't true.

* * * * *

Now we're coming to the sand. There's a new moon, "with the old moon in her arms," the one line of poetry he's recited in his life to me. I set him on the bench. We look at the water for a while. Companionable silence, is what he'd call it. Twenty minutes and he wants to "go back up" to the cabin. We do it the same way, his hands on my back, nearly weightless. I hear his feet shuffling sand, first, then grass.

* * * * *

My sons and I drove through the night, getting there. Just after dawn, when they were still asleep, I saw the highway flying backward in the side-view mirror and the mirror itself, a bright hole, dead-center in the shadow of the car.

The Last Time I Saw Him I Didn't

In the parking lot outside my dying father
air went blank. I was there, and I
would've liked to have him see me
standing there, but he couldn't stand
and I went on with standing even though
I knew that he could not. Short
and empty trees around the lot,
and at my back might have been
The City Unseen. I couldn't tell.
I might have been looking up,
sifting for his window all along
the white hospital's shut portholes
while at my back might have been

another world. But even what I could
see, those neglected trees, were not
seeing anybody off. Their hands
weren't kind of metal, sad.
From the parking lot outside
my father was invisible, although
I'd have liked to find his room and waved.
I'd have liked to see him see me
get inside the Chevy, drive away,
but he wasn't standing up and that was
that. I didn't know the window, not
for sure, counting down along the bricks
from red glass at the corner of his floor.

I couldn't find the page. He said *hope,*
I thought he smiled a lot for someone dying.
That's how he went through life,
the difference between *oh, just not this*
and *not this time.* Above the hospital
and not invisible, a plucky blackbird moved
a crow from one piece of the sky to off.

*

> But I was still the child he watched
> and I'd have liked to have him see me
> standing here. I'd have liked to have him
>   see me driving off, through
>   something halfway solid,
> to watch me going, one more time, in his car.

Lamp and Wick

Light was the thing of truth—
until the truth, as Dickinson exclaimed,
the sun that came, "in ribbons,"
up, took residence
in glass. Just

      as that look on my father's face
when he began to tell us calmly
he could see the end.
                 The look on doors

not opened many years.
Sometimes there's only one wall left
      and the farmhouse has dissolved behind it
         (although there's no *behind,*
    no room there at all).

You can stand and can't go in,
      even if you touch,
      push the door open.

Even if the single wall
holds, the window holds . . .
              * * * * * * *
then the moment when
      there's nothing left unsaid.

there's nothing left to add, really.
              * * * * * * *
to sit and wait.
              * * * * * * *
and darkness when it comes is honest dark.

The Night You Thought to Stop

Stately rain, little mouths
rushing to the darker mouths of grass.

The great mouth, later,
stars that were not mouths, a parent's mouth
that, kindly, wouldn't stop, the yellow wall
that opened slowly, hair
and hands like whipping flags.

One vase at the end of either wrist,
the fallen rain that caught on thorns,
rose stems in the window light,
straw the sheep had torn
softly from my hand, a window
like the mouth of someone's cave.

The mouths of birds
singing when the sun dissolved.

My mouth in the mirror, tiny elevator
praying to my face:
whose funny idol,
agates where the eyes went
striped with mercy, disregard?

My entire face,
a mouth

and then the moon,
kissing at my skin, bone-white.

A letter I no longer had to write,
the pen, its lips
a little barrel, slipping from my hand

*

waterfall, a waterfall,

the mouths of stones on shore,
the sun, again, a tongue
pushing from inside the sea.

Shadow

Patch of night, shade from some big doll's eclipse,
spy cooked up on cocaine
and running guns to the other side. Contract.
In this universal: the particular,
a little smack of death, big leaves, that shade-loving
plant. Here's memory, clothed.
Here the fur shaved off to club the poodle's legs,
and in the pile of newsprint
dripping off the paper tossed through rain against the steps

I've fallen to but do not lie
against, all the news of fire spreading, trees that rise up,
phoenix, from their dark lakes,
their shadows out in public, Elvis imitators, all bad satin
and his wrap-arounds.
When we began to pull the blinds down?
When we began to squint?
Naked cousin to mirage, nuance, color's ghost,
I sign to you because we stocked the shelves

together, once, used the sticky gun when prices were reduced,
because in school you'd complain
so constantly, in silence, how copies ruled the halls. To you
because you've moved along
inside my gloom or joy, as someone constant. Since at night
you deepen, bulk into the size
of space. Because you are imperfect. Since you follow me.
Because, on too-bright mornings,
I'm willing now to see the one I can't become.

The Other Biography

It would still rain, there, and time would find a way to grind
daylight into powder.

From that powder, one step more to blue that blots a canvas, blue
of stolen jewelry, blue of keys,

blue of one stocking. Where afternoon will fracture
backwards, toward the noon

of *almost was,* the earth rolls out beneath an elbow to a backdrop
built from wish,

horizon no one notes, a book we've fallen into, falling into sleep
before. We brush our cheeks,

rub eyes against the pivot we have made, heels of our hands,
not as ritual, but with the force

of driving tung oil into wood, the branch of someone's arm,
sanded down to nearly smooth

as what I touched but could not hold, someone keen, someone
I felt, once, stepping out of me.

Sunburst, Rush Hour

Nothing unless something burns. Rust, even.
It wouldn't have to be this scorching blue, this light
Shot through with light. The tales might begin
In darkness, unto darkness then return,
But there's no story to it all until this thing—
This *light!*—opens up the stage. Fires have been set,

Signal, seed and molten core and wave and wave of it,
This great destruction raying out at once, the gold
And yellow into white, this driving through a needle's eye
From spectrum into blinding nowhere. All across
The dictionary, off the page like pre-Columbus glory,
Light simmers as the thinnest fabric we can wear.

Take it in a little at the shoulders, as cars do
Stopping off the Interstate because the sun is punching out
For the day so brilliantly. *Glory* as a parasol,
A weed in our blood. A voice inside a white coat tells you
What you had is going nowhere, it's defunct.
You think *I will live,* and live you yet

Though breathing it is harder to recall *resplendence.*
These *re-* words, they'll drive a body nuts:
Redo or *remission.* Things stream out from centers
Where we're not for long, spoke of trees, spoke of water,
Spoke of *god-I-dodged-that-bullet:*
Then it's near impossible to say what's gone by.

It's so absurdly beautiful, this evening,
The translator has not invented *self* just yet,
We wait inside the cottage, little mice, happy with its emptiness.
And still the circuit runs from light to dark and back to light,
As if, within our thousand faces, cubists every one,
We might fix what disappears before it can be written down.

II. *Politics*

Shapes as Prologue in the Tower of London

A great iron hinge, a metal hawk
      splayed into its own shadow
on this door stapled, wood
      it's hard to tell from stone.
These bulks, stacked, these walls,
      and the chopping block, cupped

a bit, like a hand beneath a child's face,
      where the young queen set her chin:
chalice: stump. What else to justify
      this mechanism invented?
Hinge. the concept of a pin,
      the concept of an axis;

the finger and the ring; the scepter,
      gold, around which her body,
opened, then was forced to orbit.
      As this door will open, moaning
badly, brute genius. To pivot, then.
      This iron forged, given throat:

      this way into history.

Hatred:
On Returning to a Poem with Language Backwards

i.e.   I wake in solid walls of milk.   i.e.   "The Cut,"
    before they went to Spandau, got *Ballet;* that is, younger.

So: I wake younger, then the eyelid circus stops.
    I wake at 2:
    33, I wake   at 4:16 and then, again,   5:57.
    I can't   find out
    who's sending me these messages.   i.e.   *Juggler.*
Two weeks ago last   night I read: rape
    and murder,   unnamed girl,   just 14,
    who died, not   from multiple penetrations
    of her anus, mouth, vagina,   but from 4
    heart attacks she suffered over hours.

So: This morning loosed, so: *"through the mud of just*
    before dawn, white-   tailed . . . "   I can hardly read.
    And a scrap of someone saying something *"smile,*
    like a white bird."
        I know
    there is a dream I had I can't   recall,   one to carry me
    through the traffic,   i.e: *Stupid acrobat.*
    The missing dream's a little   lightness
    and a thumping, almost,   in my forehead. New
    sinus trouble.   i.e.   almost a scent too faint.

So: no trail is. And now,   as always, the music played
    backwards holds no clue: so: *" . . . deliat-etihw eht,*
    nwad erofeb tsuj   *fo dum eht hguorht"*   echoes
    "drib etihw   *a ekil, elims"* and   so what?
There's light enough to read and   I've learned how,   i.e.
    I'm 60, still   alive in this world,
etc.   with *love*   and with its palindrome

*

and so: there's light enough   to read, many
          years of it

          and I tell you here   the imagination's   worthless.

i.e.   She was 14.

i.e.   etc.

The Trickle of Blood

In the horror flicks and war novels, childbirth, *The Sporting News*—
on the elk that's hoisted up by antlers
for the outdoor page, a mouse
the mousetrap like a deck of meanest cards snapped up—
from chin, from corner of the mouth,
hooked trout's vent, gills
like coral fanned, the broken nose, vagina, split lip, knuckle, steak
inside its squeaky package. A famous warning,
horn, sounded in the Alps, a landscape
far from here as lunar. Listen: *damage* is the song that binds us.
Even if we *can* get back, even if the infant thrives,
the torn hand mends. This is how
we're haunted, indicated. This is how our building turns
a little red at sunup, even as we shove
into the river once again, we step into the day preoccupied.

Teens

One part torn stepladder, one part battered swan,
this morning—as every morning after prom—
wet with sunlight, deer lie only slightly blooded,
spread like hands with fingers broken
off the road. We've sent the young ones on their way
again, with hoopla, absurd costumes,
fabric, flowers, flavored drinks.
For a decade-and-a-half they were with us

in, at times, happiness unqualified.
This has not been true for several years,
their joys fretted more and more with worry,
thirst. It's natural enough.
Some carry in their brains small outposts
on fire already, primed with alcohol.
The landscape made of ash is open to them
like a table setting. Some love now as we did once.

Most, as always, may easily be prodded into war.

"Long War" Drone:
On a Term Proposed and Abandoned by the Pentagon

I'm making a war sandwich out of war cheese on war bread
milled by the warrior river.

I'm having a wartime beer on the war-torn front porch while jets score
blue across war-painted sky.

In the blank noon war clacks, taking off the kids like bark around a tree.

The war is building nothing but a boat that's filled with war,
going off to where war is. Out of sight. The sightless war.

Over there are faces streaked by war and war on railway tracks—
but here the billboard war, great warred-up slogans looped like flags,
bumper sticker war, magnetic ribbon war.

There's war a million miles away and war inside the sink.

There's war that's stalking up like a tattoo stand.

There's war inside the mall, there's war in shoes, in underwear,
there's war along the Interstate, war at work.

War's raining in the trees and birds like little bits of fire.

War staggers in the alleys, goes paving all the streets:
there's the radio and war, the singing war, the battle for the stars.

There's tabloid war, the diet war, war that's ground into your skin,
there's smell of war, the stink of never peace, the war that's making cash.

There's war and war: my dog's got war
against the fish, the fish got war with air.

The ground shivers just a bit—gonna' blow—volcano war, earthquake
war, the war of many floods. It's war until the end of time,
it's war and without stop.

Green and yellow, black and red, it's war with pointed hats, it's war
that's needling, war to come, it's war gone by.
Think *history of luck*—and war inks it out. The song you bubbled
in your lover's ear—and war has popped an inner tube,
it's going fast downhill to war, it's war we didn't know.
War whispers, "Stop!" but we won't come back
now. The dead are small so far away, we hear them like sunrise.
It's the sunrise war.
This sandwich has already hit the ground.

It's not sand I'm clicking my teeth on, not something on its way.

It's war, again, the bread is grit with it.

The lie of war. The old lie, war.

As scent to cut flowers, a carcass in a stream:

it's war, it's war.

It's nothing, just the war.

The First of the Month

Into the distance disappear the mounds of human heads. I dwindle—
go unnoticed now. But in the sentimental novels and in children's games
I will come from the dead to say: "the sun!"
—*Osip Mandelstam*

Once there were two empires at war, armies
dressed in blue, armies dressed in green.
A hundred generations they had struggled.
Generations. Then an eremite came clear-eyed
from the mountains, counseling the emperor of blue
to dress his soldiers green, the master of the green army
to dress his soldiers blue. But the war continued as before.

We claim the past does not exist. How then can we leave it?
Or the future isn't yet. How then do we journey there?
I say ponder death and conjure childhood long.
It's time to pay the bills, the first come round
again, all smiles and loss, the sharp grille-work
on a '50 Ford. Here's a different number
to write on all the checks, a little automatic joy

that time has moved. Here's the finest dust
and something measured, Roman, as Persephone
strode forth, hair and eyes, defiant from the shadow
we call time. Absence. There's nothing prodigal
in her return, if no one wants to know too much
what went on down there. The dark. His grasping will,
the memory that nearly leaves her face.

Drought in August

The empire starts to breathe. Octavian,
who "found Rome brick and left it marble," names this month
a chariot: bone-white horse, bone-white
plume to part the crowd. None but poor remain
in the city, roads into the Forum badly
shaded. White marble then, and *pax Romana,* with huge arms
and iron. In centuries the executions turn

quite bloody, and it's so very hot, and it's that ripe
persimmons plump and rot to honey scented
almost cinnamon, and it's the good who still die
young, if only dying makes them so,
as blessed are the poor in spirit. August: sardonyx,
its stone; the flower, poppy. Perchance, then, to dream.
But how did they go on, not knowing then the earth by rote

turns, the sun holds still? What if that great sphere of light
simply rode away into the mass of smaller faces
bearing their own darkness only wearing hats?
Disappeared it seemed for good? Wouldn't they sacrifice
the living just to get it back? I don't think *we'd* hesitate,
as I don't think the dead do not continue—but as colors.
Wisdom isn't in the eye of the beholder.

We love them and they slip, are torn away.
And we are drenched with this, as the cardinal is
deeply red. And we are black at mouth and eyes,
and all these sundry parts that must ingest this earth,
this empire that's heating now, eventually will cool.
That moves on like the spectrum gathered in this light.
Hardened. Marbled and prismatic, like Augustus great.

Smoke Love

After born-in-snow-and-nearly-Canada,   I spent ten years in red dirt,
     Dixie.   My landlord turned his furrows with a mule.
At the end of every row he lifted up the blade   and he and mule and plow
     backed around and he would shout his mule tongue   and she would
sometimes bark.   They worked askew and made me wonder how

madness finds desire.   In those days I taught my schizophrenics.
     They could write but couldn't save themselves.
They would work askew as well, though it came to nothing,
     and what they wanted badly was a hammering desire,   a list of wants
that couldn't leave off, sleepless want, missing and still missing
and the anger, then.

     Though he was a peaceful man, tools sprouted from his hands
and hands that made the plowshare made the sword,
     as any tool that we have is just a hand   refined: hammer, awl;
as there are still those few who wear a crown,
     to signify.   Their bodies don't belong to them.
They mate.   They will not stand aside.   They fight about the name:
     Sharpsburg or Antietam.   No one talks
     slowly enough.
And while it is not true that small, red flowers sprouted from the soil there,
     at the battle's end, there was a sponginess,
there were the thousands shrunk into their corpses, drained,
     the soil,   a sponginess.

Afterwards, a singing.
     Prayers to begin with and then song. The perfect lack of irony
in military graveyards.
     At first the sound was mournful.   It would take your breath, hold it
                                                             down.
You would have a hard time breathing evenly.

Only later on the songs became heroic.
     You'd see that they were tools as well, wouldn't you? I mean,
anyone would see.

You'd see in all the jewelry,   ribbon, bayonet,
drum roll and salute,   what art makes out of what it will mistake as love,
        what art will shape from these, our greatest wants gone wrong.

Paradise

How *the garden* became invisible, as
     my son is twenty, "he's his own
man," a neighbor tells me.   We are talking at a fence,
     my boy's been arrested. Not
     boy.   This took place where an alley, freighted
     with the restaurant Dumpsters,
     backs into a clutch of barrels and chain link.
There's been an exchange of blood.

                * * *

     How paradise was *garden*—red arms
with a thousand yellow hands—and the predator was nil.
     Nil the desert fox,
     nil the falcon, nil the skunk   with its triangular intentions.

What can be understood from the animal that kills
     another animal to live?
     I have killed another   animal to live?

                * * *

     But the garden was a respite and was blue
as an open hand, blue   as sleeping with the sky.

"A child," we said,
     when we turned to one another, bleary, tired
     with trying, the love we'd made from sweat and air.

                * * *

How the garden was deferred,
     how getting in became impossible,   clothed in flesh:
     the way out has never been
the way back.

                * * *

Of course there was a wall, it wouldn't be a garden
     if there hadn't been a wall, pink stone,

no sharp (yet) tatters   glass   mortared at the top, for teeth.

Cooling Tower, Smokestack

As if each tree's a wall.

Take blue and scratch *bad sky* in the sky
with a stick.

Without cloud we die (see *rain=*
crop; see *snow+*
sun=crop)

and the rain scratches but does not
crop.

The reader crops; the writer
scratches, paints.

And this smoke stacked as if
the lighthouse moved its peg leg
inland, turned to steaming.

Landscape with
tower.

So it's clear the humans have
landed, the other ships
move off—the ships
of deer, hummingbird,
the invisible ones.

They scratch something: therefore
antlers, tiny beaks.

It would not be alive, but writing, paint.
Not this atomic, ever.

Wartime Portrait, Dried Sunflowers

Here's the earth, stuck page. Here's the garden
with a nymph already stationed at the rack and screw. The whatever.
So much for nature. Now *clash* sogs the dirt.

You can feel it sponge at every step around your boots, feel it oozing up
to trees, *zig-zag,* through the porch screen.
There's no thumbing edges, no separation. Drop the book or slam

the door. Hardwood floors and house
of photographs. . . . Out here . . . death with flower heads. Not
that there's no pain in the house of photographs,

but it's a family of pain, with other things mixed in, like *love,*
responsibility. Still, *we can't get it*
right. And even if we could, grief would loom so awkwardly,

stinking up the scene in every school play: see the kids
so shock and stare? Lose a line, stammer?
Some of them will be at it longer than the rest. Artists.

Memory experts. Leaving for tomorrow everything except this blunt *lurching,*
shadow, aftertaste:
this *underneath* with no anticipation. They don't know

you put it from your mind as best you can. They don't know,
yet, the turn away, poor reason. They don't know
these hurts they have will open, will. Like seeds.

High Waves

These are full of sand and drive to froth what they carry,
like a twist of DNA, peppered carefully
      with information that concerns the color of your eyes,
      how the overhead light
      glows, just an instant,
when you shut it off and start
toward sinking into sleep.

But let's say that you're not
      going off too easily, and what you hear inside your ears, blood
      batting all its soccer balls through your crowded hallways:

Taj Mahal, that's the scene,
      knots of visitors who orbit, amble
      near the walls, and on the cool mosaic, boys,
in the endless game, kick and run and kick and run.

Though it's not endless, just widespread, as these waves
that travel from the center of their world
      to end in noise at last, strangers who collapse
      upon our doorstep, white parcels
      falling with them as they faint, and some message
none of us can read, gripped inside
      their teeth as though they smiled.

Blood Gutter

You might want to know how *tube* comes down from Latin used
                                for *leader,* moves from *conduit*
to good-old *can-do*-spirit. The tongue will gnarl and slick,
                                consonants will blur.
I do not mean that dreams still live inside a corpse:
                                it's centuries of speech, turned
like hay, over, forked to keep from breaking into fire

                                where barns are full of life,
their fixtures—mottled cats (and hidden mice)—shine like chrome
                                once the light goes off. Sundown:
it's a food thing. When they stopped their marching, Roman troops
                                would ditch the earth, build
stockades. Every day. Back home in the arena, "feral beasts,"
                                nine thousand on one afternoon,

were butchered in the great and civic lung that was the Coliseum.
                                Extinctions—Mesopotamian
lion, North African elephant—were "extensively regional."
                                No gutters on a barn divert
the rain. It's irony, that anyone's intestines should be named
                                by a term that also designates
the groove along a blade which lets the bloodstream out.

                                These ways to tackle pressure . . .
required since you'll need to stab as quickly as you can again.
                                Etymology. I'd fill my trunk with it
like the hearse we use for veterans, bristling to its silver gills
                                with yellow gladioli named
for murderous short-swords that won and kept so long
                                an imperium to rot.

Referred Pain

I do not have anyone
        sick and I do not think of the sick
much especially   not out of nowhere like
this morning walking from the parking ramp they say *structure* when it
        strikes me there
        is someone sick I should be   thinking of or going to
or thinking about seeing

So I think about the sick on   the elevator down   rows
        of possible sick my mother
when she died my father   and his stroke or friends
        I have watched   sick but none of these
is the one I am   thinking of   for no reason
        when I get off   at ground level and step outside and know
It's like it's me   in a hospital
        gown a white gown with a tired   face somewhere or someone
        like me   whose picture is so vivid I
        have to stop on the sidewalk
It's me but doesn't seem like any   me to come
        but I feel compelled
        to visit now right
now as if I've known a week
        where he's been being treated where
        he's been waiting
This is dumb I   tell myself I've work
        but I can't stop it there he is   somewhere and the urge
to touch the grass to bend
        down and just touch it makes me
        bend down   and not because it's   April
and the grass is cold or
        the earth beneath is warming
And though I am easily   embarrassed and think in
        spite of this that someone   passing
        by or what will think me odd I stoop
        here a while longer

And because this   feels like the visit I   should
     make to   him somewhere   someone
who has the same   something maybe   I don't
know but a brother who   is dying from it now

On Sound: As Sirens in *The Diary Of Anne Frank*

There is no doubt that paper is patient
—*A. Frank*

Life. I've *seen* all sorts of junk: spruce trees
shouldering their way through snow so thick
(it seems) they're moving up against the glass window
like great white bulls, to the living room that is
the inside of our eyelids, but it's black cold,

and the wind, sanding ice from off those needles,
stings and makes us crooked, Italy,
France when we were there, towers, useless
arches glommed with marble lions, spritz
and Roman numerals, the bright red, brighter

blue and cubes and wheels driving (chrome)
past the Coliseum, beetles doing Arabic
in rotting wood, tunnels, paths and vistas,
cavern darkness dark enough to see, really,
ka-zillion stars (so handy) slung above

a rock outcropping where you've staked
an orange tent, orange on its own, liver,
raw and cooked, city lights below the plane,
ectoplasm, one-celled blurbs, a thousand words
or less. But close one eye? It all goes planetarium.

Close the next, and what's left? A flat, archaic atrium
of sound. Not much, most times. More is coming,
certainly, the little hissers, clicks and *wooshings,*
creaks, the booms and bangs, and chatter-chatter,
and etc., but not too many noises here to trip on,

headstones, tree stumps, loomers in our memories.
And why? You try to count them off (I try

to count), the sounds that you recall as well
as something seen, but brain's not propped up
well enough to handle being shoved inside a box

        and left for long. Shut my eyes and instantly
        here's the center of a universal room,
        the what's behind, the sides and back and corners,
        mopboards, floors below to feel with my feet.
        I'm putting down my postcards of the stuff

I've seen out there. I'm tired thinking death is Tuesday
when it's so more nimble, silent. Quiet banshee.
I don't trust my eyes, having heard my son choking
in the green (and quick) and dimming edges of a field,
one more sound that stuck, like the steel snip cutting

        through his slick umbilical, a whitetail bluntly
        swatted off the fender, shovel cutting gravel,
        those sirens in *The Diary*. And silence coming
        back always, such a good retriever, with our faces
        as a noise hanging from its lips like any rag.

Some of Us

have not been stricken so
we've seen the little stars have
heard the small trees snapping felt black and orange earth.

Some of us haven't moved the knife
against ourselves the brain gone mannequin
silly blood the dog is lapping off the floor.

Some of us have not
counted out meticulous the pills.

Some of us have never fired a round,
waited for the squad cars,
never hit a child, taken
money for a lie, become
strangers to ourselves.

Some of us a given night have not lost hold
of sleep thought life would drive us out.
Summer and the rain.

The moon alone and beautiful, some of us have not
wished to quit on love.

Some of us have never begged to change.

Reading Tracks in Snow

Birdfoot: the wedge-headed stylus used on clay tablets,
less different from my fingertips than not. The trimmed
reeds a braided scribe scratched against papyrus. Milled

from reeds, to pulp. Or birch bark. A slurry, dried.
Paper, paper—what should I do at the thought of fire?
We've been at a war long enough it coats the land

like snow, like rumor, and somewhere once again
they are burning books, the Age of Print is coming
to an end. They are burning books with lasers,

sending books along the ether, turning words to electricity.
Children's hands are raised, like starfish in a net,
hanging at the misty roadside. Everywhere. Beachhead.

Many years ago, my father lived for eight months
in New Guinea, after washing corpses dragged from reddish surf,
off Saipan. Women threw themselves from cliff top there.

He imagined living on, having kids. I write:
four-of-clubs—four-of-clubs—four-of-clubs: a red squirrel
prints where it has gone across the snow. And mice?

As if a branch had fallen there. As if a slender branch
fell and disappeared, the imprint had been partially erased.
And then been reproduced, on empty white, in Braille.

Wrought Iron Grapes and Leaves

Wind all night. By dawn,
ice lacquers down

torn elms. The fire dogs
and grate still glow,

cold smears the glass.
Snow falters and tonight

once more will fall.
The great temptation,

winter, is not to feel,
as life depends on not feeling

suffering accumulates,
learning to defer, the ore,

crushed and melted,
cooled, the magma

hammered, scalded,
hammered down

and twisted to hard fruit?
As if rust were not

another fire, or brittle air
a fuel. As if we might

shun the widespread
hunger, live, together,

in a world like this,
if it went on endlessly.

On Reading *War and Peace*

It's been months, all winter in fact, and because I cannot read as quickly as I once did I've been reading slowly *War and Peace,* even while the snow like white sparrows in miniature dipped head and head into the ground, even while the darkness lengthened and slowly then began to brighten slightly, the sun thin, but no longer getting thinner. Not "white sparrows" probably. Nonetheless, I've plowed through *War and Peace* and I can't tell you why at my age and for the first time I am reading it, trying here to figure out what *War and Peace* has to offer me.

Henry *I-know-what-they're-thinking-even-if-they're-not-aware-they're-thinking-it-just-yet* James was right to call it "baggy," calling it a "monster," still, I've been reading every day *War and Peace* and haven't finished yet. I can't tell the characters apart that well, even if I've stopped flipping back into the back side of the book for the partly helpful *dramatis personae.* I'm past the need for several maps, but keep on checking footnotes, my next-to-nothing French. I have to say these characters seem poorly differentiated, especially by comparison to others made by other not *War and Peace* authors. But I'm still reading *War and Peace,* even while I'm trying, day-by-day, to describe for myself the differences between the very first and smallest buds on red birch or on alder now, in March. It's far from just a matter of the slightest green in leaves that can't be called leaves yet. I consult my *Field Guide* and it's not much help.

On the other hand, I got *An Atlas of the Universe* for the holiday. It has a dim pinhead of lace labeled "Milky Way" in the middle of a zillion other galaxies that look so *photographed.* How's that? So maybe I'm distracted, but I'm reading *War and Peace* more slowly, reading only several pages just before I turn the lights out now. There it is, *War and Peace,* not glowing on the bedside table, sitting in its blue dust jacket first thing in the morning.

In this fashion I've gone on, reading *War and Peace,* this book that Tolstoy wouldn't call a novel. I can't get all stirred up, there's little real suspense, the thing rolls on uphill, somehow, a rock without its Sisyphus. Unless that's me. I'm mildly keen (?) to know what will come out for people I feel interest in, the lovers, *i.e.,* and there's Napoleon against the Russian Who's-It, all the misery of history, the theories of event that Tolstoy puts forth, but I'm not too concerned to know how things will go. It's not all that dramatic.

So why I've been reading *War and Peace* as one year fades I just can't say. It's not author's purpose, whatever that might be, and I don't believe writing makes anyone immortal. It's not character and point-of-view, not entertainment, really, sympathy or boredom. Stubbornness, perhaps, but even as my reading slows, puzzled at his blunt diction—"drops dropped," when it rains—I find myself floating to an end I may not reach, an infinite regress, because this *War and Peace* gets wider as I go along, its pages drifting off like landscapes, even if a parlor's been described, a ball, a conference of war. He can spend a lot of time on one eyebrow, arched.

I'm getting confused, this frigid spring, by trees that I have named before (though always later on) by flower or by leaf. I'm looking only at the texture of the bark, the color, and these just-cracked buds I haven't bothered with before. So maybe it's nothing, this *War and Peace,* other than its size. Maybe it's the fact that it exists at all. He can spend a lot of time on one eyebrow, arched. (I know, I just said that.)

And maybe I'm too pleased I've put off reading *War and Peace* this long, put it off till 60, although I can't imagine having tried to read it thirty years ago and hanging on. Like the mouse I saw this morning in an otherwise deserted field of mud and just-new grass. It had something in its paws: a scrap of twig? I couldn't make it out. There was a big sky, huge, with some blue inside of grey, and nothing moving, just this mouse. Then there was this broadening. I could see my life, like the mouse inside the startled field, clearly, from a long way off. A huge field of broken corn and this mouse, sharply clear, but seen from miles off. Say the window of a plane. And holding on to something, I don't know. A kernel, maybe.

Lake Fogged In

In chapter one, verse one
of *The Book of Fall and Heartloss,* the world is
our old twin and blue
egg. A violet rain cascades
through once-were-trees-in-full-green, and the rain mixed
in mist as scent drifts
off a blossom. Locust, cherry. Was this
the long story of nothingness
frightened at the thought of taking human form,
or the other dream, the circle
of dissolving? Our dissolving? In gravity,
in water like this, air.
In light like this which is also dark. In blues
gone through the spectrum
of weight and lift toward. *Here* it says
we should drink of ourselves.
It says *let darkness* and this *moist breathing,*
mouthfuls *wet and shined*
go on, working like the nurse in a shuttered
ICU, cloistered, Byzantine.
Perhaps she'll know for us, because she is,
as sky here, smoked, white,
how those who sleep are not those dying,
step into this richly painted
cold, as the end of anger in dismay.

Abundance

A moment longer and it's hardly night,
barn doors slightly open in the fallen snow.
Two mares, roan and sorrel, shuffle dark,

but other stalls bloom with vacancy,
dried alfalfa, timothy. Weren't there stars,
a few, like tiny lights that monitor

screens in empty newsrooms, keyboard,
telephone? Score for strings and clarinet:
horse-hair, blackwood, fire. And indeed

the small lights go about their work unseen.
Words that left the Dalai Lama hours ago,
not arrived except in filaments, like hay

that isn't glowing—*suffering* and *joy*—
now have kept their rounds. The still-famous
"moment of silence" advances into dawn

and here, an instant, fills the yard, the shed,
the t.v.'s off and pale blue cataract before
light cracks out from scarlet night. One second:

it seems as if there's nothing lived or died.
But then it's just the sun, again blood-red,
if, as some blood, once again, the blood of life.

Saint Ophelia

The corpse floated along   its bed of ferns,
kneeler,   dock and low handrail.

I can reach her face if I wanted. If
she was her face.   I don't *prefer:*

small earth, tiny   arrows loosed
as sunlight moves off   quarters sinking

overboard, *a-glint,* and my sudden hands
      as useless to seize her as   a pair

of shoes to snatch a thin necklace. . . .
Or large earth, my   wishing   a terminal

fire, great buttressed tongues to flame
      the curtained mirror, their   intake

woosh, so   *here*   before the roar of sound.
I would think *sound,* since there is prayer

and there is the related   question: directing
      prayer. Useless prepositions. What

to or *at,* or *in,*   or   *out,* or *by,* or
through?   I mark every day

a few of us long untouched.   There are
      men and women walking now

alive that no one's touched in more
than a year at all. These

undrowned. With a patroness and
      is that some—*what?*—   radiance

III. *Age*

Dispatch

Say you've come in a stream to the end of the sun.
    the children you have sent on, like colored sound,
        and you find yourself without them.
they have burned off,
        as fog burns off a valley, heat
        rises off of stones.
    how clearly now their faces disappear
    inside their faces disappearing:
        daughter to woman, son to man.

    say the long hallway had fewer doors,
    the long city from which you disembarked,
        like a cloud that leaves the sky,
            was a city empty
            in the hour before dawn,
        with wind that wore its wrappings loosely and birds stare.

    say that you have counted joy
                and numbered sorrow.

    say that you have lived beyond your calling,
        the ground on which you stood is cut away:

        I send you, friend, my greetings.

Cloak

Another of the disappearing words, as if forests walked
        to a great hilltop, were transported upwards.
Not into the clouds that also leave the sky, touched

with rose, a little gold, but the way that language has
        with extinction: *cloak,* once a symbol made from *dignity,*
a word also cloaked. A sheath and some protection,

a thief inside a shadow—*cloak*—someone covered,
        deep in knowledge that belongs to her alone.
Threat, disguise, *cloak* like green that climbs through grass.

Cloak could thrive on contrast: black and yellow, blue
        and white, brown and almost red, a robin's brighter
down marking off *below,* or the pale underbelly, camouflage,

but the shape of *someone-in-a-cloak* also disappears.
        From the precipice it shifts through those trees vanishing
although it's wide daylight. Nonetheless. Better to be gone,

if even then there's wind sometimes we need: as someone
        loving touches you, not to take you in, fingertips,
but drifts along your cheekbone with her nails.

Ghost Pain

You can sit at this table if you want
though most of us are missing arms or walk
the house the wasp-thin hall
the dust if it strikes you

The lamps do antler and the siding nails

Most of us are old enough
but that truth changes sheets and glides
through everyone

Perhaps these windows suit
you the sun or the moon's neck

We have not been able to fix that
but we talk we
point and memory evokes as if
you were to carve wax
in the shape of the wind

Cut it off somewhere
it don't stay cut off long
or *take the hand emerges from the smoke*

The night has dropped a wreath around the lake

Find water find it going
green awhile drive
the spike or pull it out she tells me
and it sounds true

As it does when someone says
show you to the door

After AA, the Somnambulist Dream Again

There are eyes like hard boiled eggs hanging from their branch tips, eyes like chairs around a kitchen table when the table's gone. In The Eye Museum, life-sized models, Cro-Magnon eyes in glass, and the eye-feeling beaming out from a swatch of rubber grass, the plastic rocks displayed.

Eyes in knots of wood, in floated bubbles, triangles, eyes inside their corners like the catfish head, the eyeball on the pyramid inside a dollar bill. The eyeball of the wooden knob at the stair rail's end, the eyeball in the open palm, the period.

Here's the city limits. There's beyond, with its trees and mice, there's the life I left behind, where I'd be slumped across a drink, a beer-slicked floor, bleared and private, mad. It seems that I'd been happy, once, just a while ago. That life, then. But take the picture from its frame—a bowl of mute apples, a mess of zinnias, flipping up, like cheerleaders, exploding with their sexual importance for a team, made of light, that crashes at the trim of darkness—and hang the empty frame on its nail in the wall: what is not a picture?

How might I comprehend, in something like this stillness and its keen reductions, my self, locked up, on guard in the slowly melting head of the comet of my life? How contend with, once foreseen, this square, pacific darkness recommending—in the blur and mild bewilderment before I can assign to that blue panel on the wall *only glass and moonlight;* to that tiny eye, electric and now red, *just the clock alarm*—my last breath, that gradual outburst beginning with the eyes and dropping to the finally-and-forever-open lips, as that breath leaves, walking out on me, smaller, getting smaller as it goes?

No one's talking now, in a company of strangers I have known many years, with saucers and the thin delight of coffee: spoons to *ping* against the plain ceramic cups and ring, the small weight of the spoon that carries to your wrist, dipping with a spoon, down into the cup, the little, submarine a-blossoming of half-and-half, the steam, signaling: *we're still alive. we're over here. alive.* And then to stir. It's merely blunt darkness, in a bedroom I don't recognize for an instant, rising out of sleep, and the premonition of a night when I'll have started toward a last negotiation, footsteps I have heard in the subway tunnel, diminishing, unseen.

Recovery

for M.B.

They tipped back their frozen shoes, drank seal's blood.
      But not that red.   More a shade of rust.

Their ship was locked in ice. A man has written
      he will cut off fingers he can't feel   and eat them but he dies.

Don't tell me that he can't guess what privation is.
      Here's the blindfold, girl and wooden shack.   The microphones

will snake, later, down. Rescue and what fact brought home?
      That light *is* blinding.   Of all the colors

we can see, it is yellow carries farthest across the arctic shield,
      lens. As flashbulbs now,   the odd birdsong for her had been.

Mist

Dull sky, beach and mist—on Titan it's raining methane,
but here there are the thousand shades from *lavender*

to *violet,* the gray *flowering,* the gray as *land,* the gray
as *foliage,* the gray as *filling sky.* There is the gray beneath

waves, the gray fish drawing through its gills a molecule
from one who drowned off a junk, went down with a galleon.

Those *are* pearls that were. . . . *Gray eyes. You there, shade.*
We're taught that fire sits a shoulder opposite from water:

it's fire that's prophetic; water that endures. This is not true
sometime afterward, as you've learned from love or anger,

as the taxidermist knows the glass set into plastic sockets
in the buck's head cannot see but is a window nonetheless.

Into *remains.* Into *what persists.* As this bluish sand persists
through gray, as this leafy fog that might have sprung from limbo.

Straddling a shoreline, foot in surf and foot on earth,
who has not become the great Colossus miniscule?

Even if this rain, even if this air we breathe so casually—
this moiled air—on another world might instantly ignite.

Path in Sand, with Hawthorn

Into the woods in a cut of light, as if through drawn blinds,
and a hanging gate of dead branches, a wooden hand
lying on a tablecloth in some reconstruction: *The Pilgrim Home.*

There's nothing left of what is not included. Red birch
twist a little slowly overhead, archway, and I feel as I felt
last night, sitting in the high school auditorium, spying down
on boys and girls singing like a pack of birds, black shadows
singing, white blouses. Life has these telescopes.

Landscape or singing kids: they can back-peddle so quickly,
a camera that's wheeling, rearing up on a wedding,
horse that tears across the beach in every movie about love
before there were electronics. But not this life, not mine.

I don't mean *might-have-been.* I mean the great smallness
of a year, a decade. The powerful need *to comprehend.*

For what? Death is at the beach and dumb as mystery,
a grief I can't walk up to, an empty house, gables dim.

The sand as well goes singing off to somewhere green and dark,
and here's this uphill afternoon where, at my back, the water is
sounding nothing, as they say, like applause. Not that.

Walking on Water

It is true *the sky*
clings to the earth. As

if it could fall. And
we live *within.* It
is different on
* * * *
Mars, for instance: where
ice sublimes to gas,
to water *vapor*

immediately.
There are no shapes there
* * * *
that rise from water
and, *as we do, from*

themselves, before
they collapse, return.
This explains why it
* * * *
is important to
know (*what ever we*
might be when we are

not alone) what is not
or with us when we are.

Torch

Red breath, shoe made from your old shoes, child of your hand and eye—

defunct as Olympus, movie-set stem and vase, I've gone pale

in the glare of electricity. Down a hall in this museum I see ancestors—

flint and scrap of iron. Where once I multiplied, I dim—

where once I dimmed, I am not. As I am not the sconce or branch, pitch-soaked

rag and distaff. Only simple need, called up by the dark which is no more—

that first darkness—to the brilliant hand—to the helpless eye.

On Translucence

As the blade of a sickle finely honed,
as a newborn's skin, or grafted after fire.
A granite headstone not yet spotted
by lichen, bleared with rain and rain.
A fresh maple leaf, held between the eye
and sun, little different from my aging hand.
Ice, moonlight. The blue-wrapped Virgin's face
haloed in a fresco on a monastery wall
outside Perugia, the egg yolk sheen
painted just a year before, at noon,
the Black Plague stumbled off a ship in Sicily.

An Ordinary Day not Red

and overwrought. I felt inside my body
        like someone on a growing staircase,
mist, the day all one substance,
        softness at the throat, no sun.
Is there a face beautiful

        but without eyes? Ask the cat
and she will say the mice wear heavy shoes.
        There are my sons, the scissors
and the brush. There is my daughter,
        the rope. I planned to care for them

identically, but love will shape us
        varied instruments, as wind vs.
fire and earth. And so I seemed all morning
        part of someone's landscape,
whose I cannot say: as a ghost is not a being

        so much as it's the shape
we've said an absence takes,
        a missing key is not a missing shoelace,
though both can tell us that they are,
        that they exist, simply in our missing them.

But these do not say "where."
        They have no gravity, but hold
as does a web, its empty diamonds,
        just what make it lovely, functional,
as the deadly that today I have not missed.

Terrestrial

My dog trots grass. Her way is the way of trotting grass,
   just as air's the way of birds,

the way of air-souls, of birds who die, becoming air.
   Try imagining a fish

working hard to think of water! Creatures easily will do
   as they're made to do.

After college, I stopped saying *world* at the sight of my own blood,
   until I'm no one and his dog, as you are.

Yet we may stalk as readers through this earth, each day a page
   spread out in cloud

and building, tree or sand. And so I may be done at last:
   stretched from fear toward joy.

Not the Quick

Not the icicle, air-splitting
        root. Not
the cavern where stalactites thumb.
        Not these, slow,
since *slow* is also *close,*

but the sudden, static sparks
        in a sweater that my wife strips
off, the bedroom dark. The home
        is larger than the house.
Or those same tats of electricity

I see, kneeling on the stairs
        this morning, before dawn,
rushing through the dog's fur
        behind my hand. So *quick*
is always *far,* the caribou

that flock and run inside
        the shadow of the helicopter
blades. I've been told my nerves
        snap a charge
from tendril across synapse.

I believe these things therefore
        unseen, as if each question
I have asked and do not know—
        droplet, ash—
turns in time to this jangling.

Ash

Modicum, insoluble,   the dog rolls back her eyes to see
where they first spun   from, budding off the bulb of cells

dividing, as if to trace   a music, lifting
like a train of dark bubbles, back   down into the darker throat

of a piccolo.   Her brain stem. These friends
I should not make from animals,   whose dying is this mute.

Lullaby

Crescent of two lives come down to here:
the hand that cups the breast, the crescent of the eyes, closed,

the pursed mouth. What dark toys the moon neglects.
In bare trees, a net of light; in the woman nursing, blood.

What child is this inhaling shadow, drinking in
the mother, even as she sleeps, even as she doesn't

      dream yet: *daughter:* then, *to circulate.*

Shore As Body

The horizon washes its feet. One step more

and it could arch or crumble, but here's the earth
as it got tired and drops to sleep and this horizon

is swept clean. If there were palms, we could
put a hand out, but here are pine trees, little
webs of shadow, bits of night stuck

to the fingertips of everything—even one cloud
coming up like someone's arm hanging off
a sofa. I don't believe it's rain. And you might

lie down here as well, the sand carry you along

on its tiny, different hands, as someone diving
from a stage is carried overhead, across

a swollen crowd. The way we were carried,
wife. By one another, years gone past.
Then the ocean of our own applause

dropped off, music turning down into the lull
of wave on wave. The sweet is not the loud.

Love, what joy I know I've borrowed from your store.

Ink Drawing

The line is everything. My wife asleep
on her side thirty years, and not:

as the sound of words comes to naught.

Nothing in itself, the line describes
the poorly understood. As *I love you.*

On paper feigning space ink defines

by drawing out—the scratch of nib,
the digging in—shadows that the light creates.

What has puzzled me. What I can't take

back, take in, face on. At my wrist,
near cross-hatching, there curves

this articulate dark. I believe

in putting down the dream of gaudy color.
It won't sense how shadow puts to rest

the line, which teeters at a place cohabited
by what exists and not. It's all I have

to tell me one thing from the next,

every object so infused with its own night,
a line drawn forth from the silence that it serves.

All Souls' Morning

Before dawn, a killing frost,
  and in the dark almost beginning now to glow,

silver-beaten ragweed, silvered mullein and grass:

cold jewelry and vault, half moon, turned down
  in the center of the sky—a spray of stars.

  Only on the also cold, lunar globe

of the water tower that I cross beneath,
  the dimmest reflection: sunlight.

  November, planetary month, nothing here celestial

or cosmic—smaller landscape.
  The cold that's on its way, the cold

  that last week in this field I could not imagine,

as now I can't imagine striding naked into water
  underneath the sun.

  In this shifted world, only elemental colors

glow, colors even now
  bent across the visor of an astronaut in space.

On Plato in December after Dark

OK. There was a mirror hung to gap-toothed rock
      along the back side of the cave by sinew
      twist and spike and breadth

of vanity. Such marriages: strict
      economy. Say it was a piece of snowshoe
      hare, used to hold the femur to the hip,

but he didn't make a snowshoe, hadn't seen
      the snow. Say he watched himself
      age, instead, and he was he and was becoming

something else, he never looked into
      the grass bent down at paw and curved
      and lined into a cup of young.

Say that scrap of ligament was the very last
      to give way, in the bone centerpiece
      that had been a rodent's scaffolding

before the talon-spangled hawk broke off its life.
      From invisible connections. In the old folks' home,
      say even this one still insists that he is yet himself

though he cannot tell his son trudging through
      this blizzard, in a fur-like hat and wool, to see him
      now: he does not know the once-familiar hand.

Stippling, Winter: Letter to a Tropical Mind

Long grasses gone
to palomino. Days grown short.
As if *to diminish,*
to turn away can be *nourish.* Not tightening,
but slackened time, as
the appaloosa standing in this first snow, spot on spot, light
and dark and circle within
circle, relaxes entirely toward what I'd say was going to be
a colder time and dark, but
you are dressing all my words in your memories of them,
so how explain? There is
the half-dappled horse and these white discs whirring so
slowly it seems gravity's turned
down, is off somewhere, looking at rooftops, wistful
and a little bit 1800s.
That century, sepia, as we've read about it, or uncolored
photographs we've seen.
Maybe it *is* true, *appaloosa* means to you next to nothing,
like *tyrannosaur, arctic*
daylight, the words a four-step sound and naught.
With *Tallapoosa, Apalachee.*
Maybe you don't note the grasses going into colors found
in yellow stone, snow's not
on the menu in that hemisphere your eyes take in, has not alighted,
toe down first and, step by step,
melted on your face and hands. Maybe I am writing to you
where you always live, equator
out of which the days do not get longer or go short, darken.
Perhaps you haven't worshipped
animals, but there is one, just here, spotted in the evening sky,
out of which this perforated white,
the size of your thumbnails, nearly weightless, drifts. It's colder
than it was. The horse breathes,
does not move. It's standing like your heartbeat but completed.
We can't hear breathing, but can see,

as if there were a fire within, the horse's nostrils, smoke.
We can't hear much of anything,
in this muffled white, even if it all gets dark and darkness clears
to stars that look as cold, are said to burn.

No Postcard from a Snowfield

There is no moon.   It's black.
If you were here   you could reach through it

all the way   to some other star:
that would be a coldest trip   as well.

There are seven deer struggling   out of Douglas
fir onto the less dark   field. A churning.

There is nothing else   moving any human
eye might see.   It is extremely dark and very

cold   and seven deer struggle from the firs
onto the snowfield under   brutal stars. Alright,

the stars are not brutal,   but they lend no heat.
There is no scrap of heat no thin   paling, shred,

flag or wisp of what   we might call heat.
Unless the dim engines   these deer are

with their slender legs, plumes   of steam and iced
muzzles. That   they make little noise.

That we would   say the cold   is bitter
unless, that is, we were not   here. As I am not

now, as you are not. As   we won't ever be.
Say no one   has been here   in this cold, seen

these deer. I mean ever.   I mean the countless
times that this has   been, deer

stepping through deep snow from   woods
into an open field,   deepest night.

84

*

We have never been here.   Not in *this* world,
    going on   inhuman with its living like these deer.

After White-Out

In this field with my head
        bowed   ,is nothing
        but my shadow and the snow   .Even here ,skin
        blistered
by the sun .Off in the middle distance ,the universal
        city   glistens under gauze   ,wound
filled with its galaxy   of fires
                                .Augustine was
wrong :there's no God
in town   .Nothing but the human wisp :God
reduced to notion   ,code   ,the butt of some concealed
        weapon or better love   .Here is cold
established   ,and my shadow long
in front of me   ,swinging   ,dumbly rocketing
this bullet-nosed self   image ,black
on white ,thumbprint   gaited   awkwardly
        against a soundless   void
        ,this bright   negation
                        .There's an *I*
        within the self   ,like this   almost
blinding   blank   and stillness
        .Beyond observation ,it can't itself observe
           .A root   that cannot see .Beyond
that self   we may only stand and gape
        .Where   I'm never   ,not
        . This   the mystics have   named bliss

86